Applied ESL
Life Skills Student Workbook 3

Dara K. Fulton

Applied ESL Life Skills Student Workbook 3
Copyright © 2024 all rights reserved

Purpose of this workbook

The purpose of this workbook is for students to practice what they learn via video lessons and/or tutoring sessions. This workbook is a continuation of the Applied ESL Life Skills student workbooks 1 and 2 focusing on life skills and everyday English. Each exercise and activities are selected from topics based on lessons. Activities range from grammar, spelling, and vocabulary practice to reading and writing comprehension. Each activity is based on real-life scenarios that students can apply in their daily life. This workbook is not based on a particular English level. Instead, the lessons and exercises offer students an opportunity to review and practice their English skills.

Who is Dara K. Fulton?

Dara is the founder and ESL teacher of Applied ESL. Applied ESL is an online English tutoring service with a creative approach that helps adult learners build confidence while improving their English speaking skills. Her tutoring company focuses on the basic and intermediate levels of the English language through conversation, listening, and pronunciation practice with the use of visuals and real life scenarios. The goal is to help students feel confident to speak English in everyday life. Dara has years' experience teaching English as a Second Language (ESL) to adults. She is passionate about teaching and helping people.

Dara likes to tell her students, "Try your best."

Table of Contents

Preview

Units

Appendix: Grammar points, vocabulary word definitions, answers to exercises, and worksheets

Preview: Alphabet and Numbers

The Alphabet

A a	B b	C c	D d
E e	F f	G g	H h
I i	J j	K k	L l
M m	N n	O o	P p
Q q	R r	S s	T t
U u	V v	W w	X x
Y y	Z z		

Numbers (1-10, 20-100)

One 1	Two 2	Three 3	Four 4	Five 5	Six 6	Seven 7	Eight 8	Nine 9	Ten 10
Eleven 11	Twelve 12	Thirteen 13	Fourteen 14	Fifteen 15	Sixteen 16	Seventeen 17	Eighteen 18	Nineteen 19	Twenty 20
Twenty-one 21	Twenty-two 22	Twenty-three 23	Twenty-four 24	Twenty-five 25	Twenty-six 26	Twenty-seven 27	Twenty-eight 28	Twenty-nine 29	Thirty 30

Forty 40	Fifty 50	Sixty 60	Seventy 70	Eighty 80	Ninety 90	One-hundred 100

Calendar

January 2024

Sunday	Monday	Tuesday	Wednesday	Thursday	Friday	Saturday
	1	2	3	4	5	6
7	8	9	10	11	12	13
14	15	16	17	18	19	20
21	22	23	24	25	26	27
28	29	30	31			

A calendar shows the month, year, days of the week, and dates.

Days of the week

Monday
Tuesday
Wednesday
Thursday
Friday
Saturday
Sunday

IMPORTANT! There are 7 days in a week. Monday to Friday is called *weekdays*. Saturday and Sunday are called *weekends*.

Abbreviations for days of the week

Monday	Mon
Tuesday	Tues
Wednesday	Wed
Thursday	Thurs
Friday	Fri
Saturday	Sat
Sunday	Sun

Months of the year

January	July
February	August
March	September
April	October
May	November
June	December

IMPORTANT! There are 12 months in a year.

Dates

February 2024

Sunday	Monday	Tuesday	Wednesday	Thursday	Friday	Saturday
				1	2	3
4	5	6	7	8	9	10
11	12	13	14	15	16	17
18	19	20	21	22	23	24
25	26	27	28	(29)		

What is today's date?

Today is **Thursday, February 29.**

When we are saying the <u>date</u>, it is the ***day, month, and number*** of that day.

We also include the <u>year</u>: Today is **Thursday, February 29, 2024.**

There are different ways of writing dates

- Thursday, February 29, 2024 (day, month, date, year)
- 2/29/2024 or 2/29/24 (month, date, year)
- 2-29-24

*In some countries, the date looks like this: 29/2/2024 (date, month, and year)

*A **leap year** means when there's an extra day in a month. 2024 is a leap year because in February there are 29 days in the month instead of 28 days.

Ordinals

Ordinals are numbers that are in a series of numbers. For example: **1st (first), 2nd (second), 3rd (third), 4th (fourth)**

The 'st' 'nd' 'rd' and 'th' means the place that number is within a series of numbers

February 2024

Sunday	Monday	Tuesday	Wednesday	Thursday	Friday	Saturday
				1	2	3
4	5	6	7	8	9	10
11	12	13	14	15	16	17
18	19	20	21	22	23	24
25	26	27	28	29		

We use ordinals when saying the date.
Example: Today is Thursday, February **29th**.

Ordinal numbers

First 1st	Second 2nd	Third 3rd	Fourth 4th	Fifth 5th
Sixth 6th	Seventh 7th	Eighth 8th	Ninth 9th	Tenth 10th
Eleventh 11th	Twelfth 12th	Thirteenth 13th	Fourteenth 14th	Fifteenth 15th
Sixteenth 16th	Seventeenth 17th	Eighteenth 18th	Nineteenth 19th	Twentieth 20th

IMPORTANT!

Zero (0) is not an ordinal number. After numbers 1, 2, and 3, all numbers will end in 'th'. Example: Twenty-first (21st), Twenty-second (22nd), Twenty-third (23rd), Twenty-fourth (24th)…Thirtieth (30th), Thirty-first (31st).

Seasons

Seasons are different types of weather in a year. In many places there are 4 seasons: **winter**, **spring**, **summer**, and **fall** (also called *autumn*).

Winter

Spring

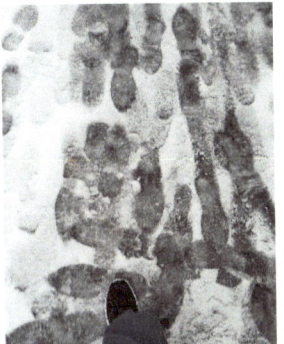

Summer

Fall (Autumn)

How is the weather today?

Weather is how the day feels (hot, cold, wet, or dry) and the temperature of the day.

Temperature is the measure of hot and cold. It is in degrees either in Fahrenheit or Celsius.

*Depending on the country, temperature will be in Fahrenheit or in Celsius.

Example: The weather today is 40 *degrees Fahrenheit*. It is *cold* and *wet* outside.

How is the weather?

It is <u>**sunny**</u>.

It is <u>**cloudy**</u>.

It is **snowy**. It is **rainy**.

Colors

We have many different colors. These are the most common colors.

What color (s) do you like? _____

What color (s) don't you like? _____

Holidays

Holidays are special occasions we celebrate during the year. Each country has their own holidays. These are some holidays that are popular in the United States.

January

New Year's Day (Jan 1st)

Chinese New Year (Jan-Feb)

February

Valentine's Day (Feb 14th)

May

Memorial Day (May 31st)

July

Independence Day (Jul 4th)

September

Labor Day (First Monday in Sept.)

October

Halloween (Oct 31st)

Halloween (Oct 31st)

November

Thanksgiving (between Nov 22nd to 28th)

December

Christmas (Dec 25th)

New Year's Eve (Dec 31st)

Birthday: The day a person is born. We celebrate birthdays in many ways. The most common way is by eating cake, going out with family or friends, and receiving flowers or gifts.

When is your birthday? _____

Time

Time is the hours and minutes in a day. There are 5 time periods in a day: **morning**, **afternoon**, **evening**, **night**, and **midnight**.

AM: morning
PM: afternoon, evening, and night

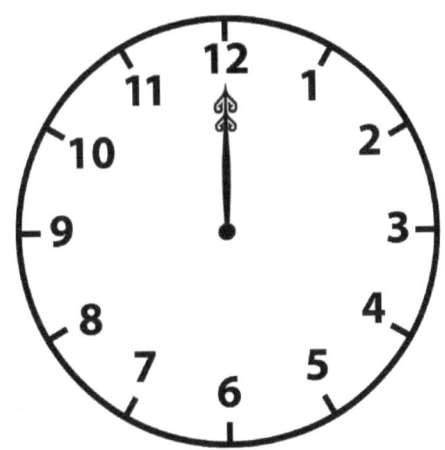

Twelve is special because it is the *start* and the *middle* of a day
Example: 12 midnight: morning (start of a new day)
12 noon: afternoon (midday, middle of the day)

We write 12 am for midnight and 12 pm for afternoon.

How do we say the time?

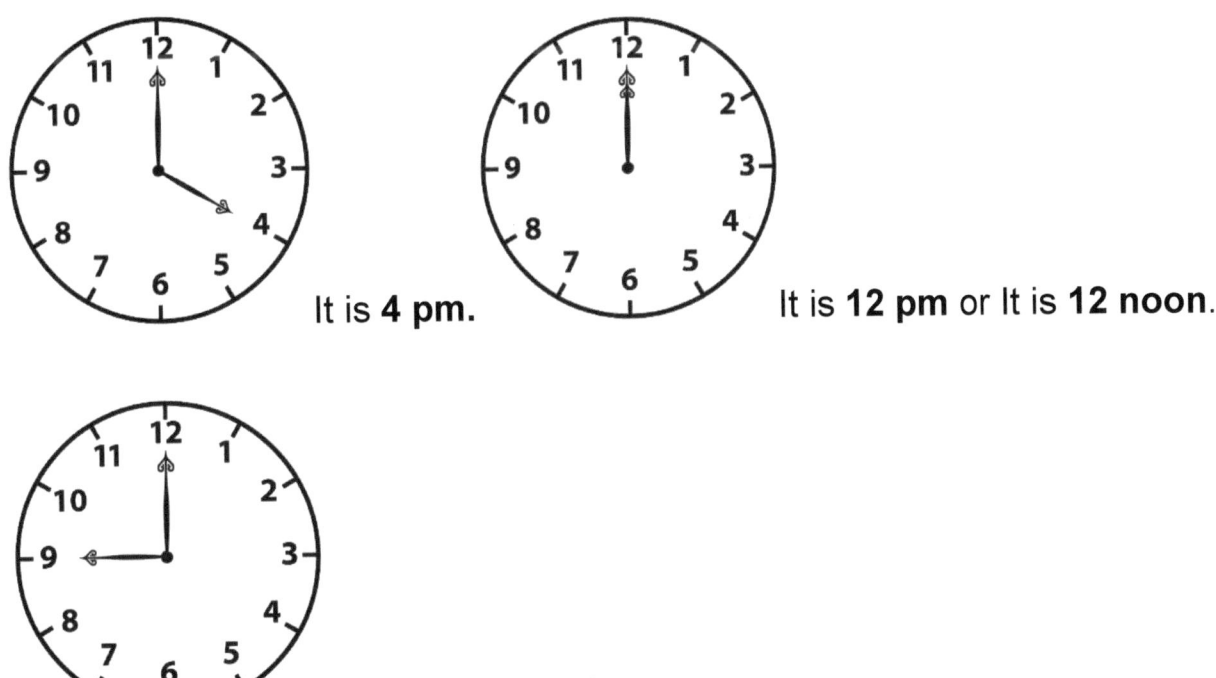

It is **4 pm.**

It is **12 pm** or It is **12 noon**.

What time is it? _____

Formal and Informal English Greetings

What is the difference between formal and informal English greetings?

Formal English conversation is to speak in an official way using correct grammar and sentences. We speak formal English to people we usually don't know.

Example: Hello, how are you?

Informal English conversation is to speak in a free, relaxed way. It does not follow the correct rules of English. We speak informal English often and to people we know.

Example: Yo, what's up?

Both of these *greetings* mean the same thing. A **greeting** is the first, polite thing to say to someone.

How do you say hello?

We say hello in many INFORMAL ways. Some of the words we use are called <u>slang</u> because it's very informal and used to speak to people we know.

Formal	Informal
Hello	Hey
*Hi	Yo
How are you?	What's up?
How are you?	What's good?
How are you?	What's up with you?

*Hi is both formal and informal

Read the conversations

Formal

A: Hello, how are you?

B: I am fine, and you?

A: I'm okay.

Informal

A: Hey! What's up?

B: Hi, I'm good. You?

A: I'm chillin'.

We have informal ways of responding to greetings. We use *I'm* for informal responses.

Formal Response	Informal Response
I am (I'm) fine	*I'm good I'm alright
I am (I'm) happy	*I'm cool I'm chillin'
I am (I'm) okay	Nothing much
I am (I'm) tired	I'm sleepy
I am (I'm) so-so	I'm meh

*I'm *good*, *alright*, *cool* and *chillin'* are used for saying I'm fine or I'm happy

Chillin' is very informal

Nothing much means nothing is happening or everything is okay

Meh is the same as so-so, which means not good or not bad

New York City Slang

What is slang?

Slang is informal English but more informal by the way we say words, expressions, and their meanings.

Slang is often considered "broken English" because it is how someone speaks it. The spelling of some slang words is not correct (example: chillin' instead of chilling).

Slang is spoken in different countries, cities, and neighborhoods. In New York City, USA there are many slang words and expressions. There are slang words used in each neighborhood of New York City!

New York City Slang Words and Expressions

What's up with you? (How are you? or Are you okay?)

 **I got you.** (I am here for you.)

 **You frontin'** (You are trying to impress others, not being honest)

 **Don't sleep** (Pay attention)

 **Nah, I'm good.** (No, I'm fine.)

 **You feel me?** (Do you understand me? or Do you believe me?)

Do you know any slang words?

Write them here: _____

_____

DARA SAYS!

- ❖ Only use informal greetings to people you know or to someone who greets you informally. Informal greetings can be impolite to some people.
- ❖ Sometimes we use body language to speak informally. Body language means to use your body to speak. For example: waving
- ❖ Body language can help you feel confident to speak informal English.
- ❖ We use different slang words when talking to friends. For women, we say **sis** or **girl**. For men, we say **bro**, **hommie** or **my G**. My G means close friend.
- ❖ Only use these words to people you know. Some people may be offended if you call them *sis* or *hommie*.
- ❖ Attitude comes with using slang or informal English. The way you say these words and your body language, will make the communication clearer.
- ❖ In New York City, people appreciate it when you try to use slang or informal English. This is an easy way to help you practice your English, and feel comfortable talking to people.

Inside a House

What is a house?
A house is a place to live

Matching: Match the pictures with the correct word

| a. Refrigerator |
| b. TV |
| c. Table |
| d. Chairs |

_____   _____   _____

Parts of a House: Where is the kitchen?

Entrance (Door)	Living room	Kitchen
Bathroom	Bedroom	Bedroom

Prepositions of place: directions; shows where things are located

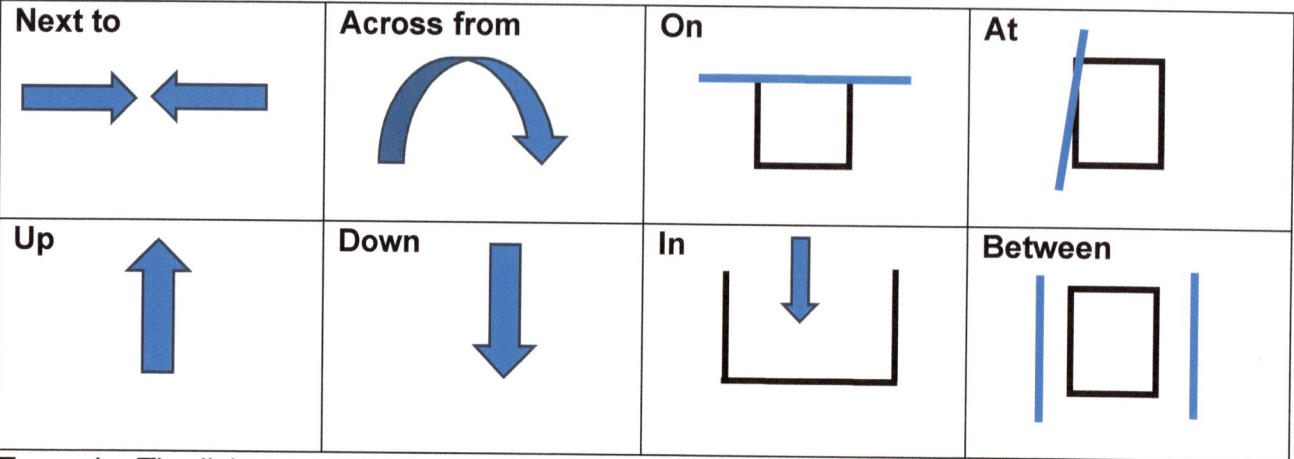

Next to	Across from	On	At
Up	Down	In	Between

Example: The living room is *next to* the kitchen.

Look at the chart and answer the questions

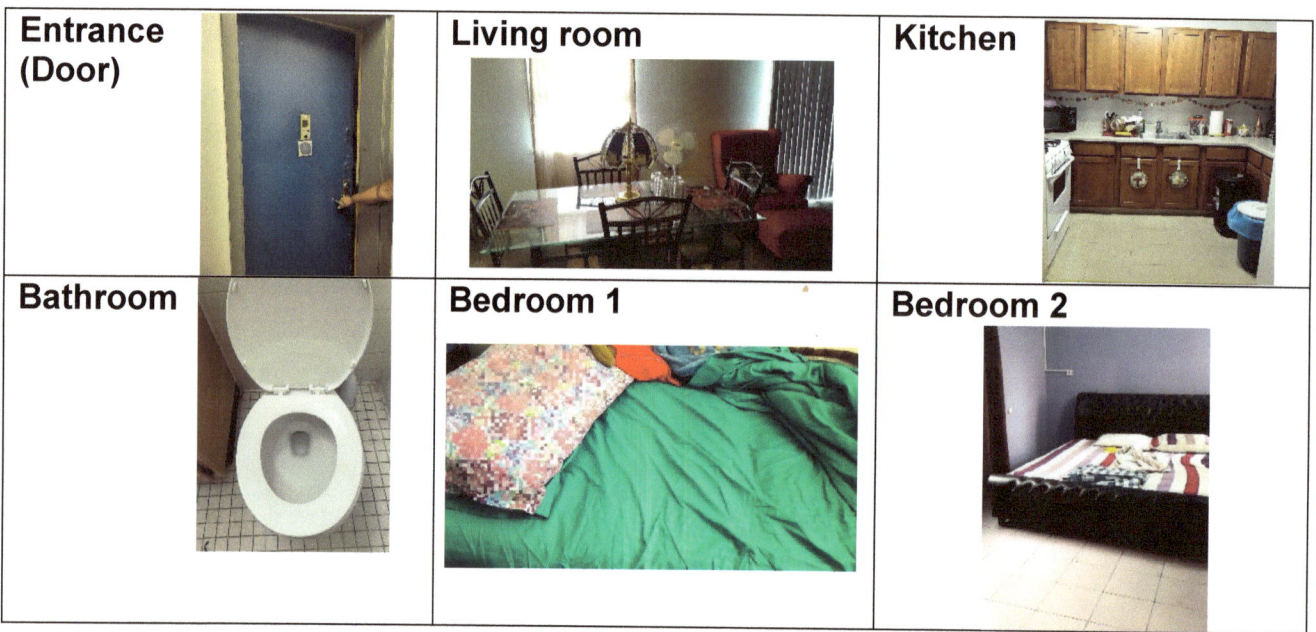

Entrance (Door)	Living room	Kitchen
Bathroom	Bedroom 1	Bedroom 2

1. Where is the entrance? _____

2. Where is the kitchen? _____

3. Where is the bathroom? _____

4. Where is bedroom 2? _____

Vocabulary

Entrance: the door to enter inside a place

Living room: a place to relax, eat, or watch TV

TV (television): something to watch shows or movies

Kitchen: a place to cook food

Refrigerator: an appliance to keep food cold

Table: a place to sit at

Chair: a seat with four legs to sit on

Bathroom: a place to relieve yourself, wash

Toilet: use to relieve yourself

Bedroom: a place to rest or sleep

Bed: to sleep

Excuse me, where is your bathroom?

Read the conversation and answer the questions

Daisey: Hey girl, I love your house!

Sasha: Thanks! Can I get you anything?

Daisey: May I have a glass of water?

Sasha: Sure.

Daisey: Oh, where is your bathroom?

Sasha: Walk *down* the hallway and the bathroom is on the *left*.

Daisey: Thanks, I'll be right back.

Where is Daisey? _____

What did Sasha give to Daisey? _____

Daisey needs to go to the *bathroom*. Where is it?

_____

What does *I'll be right back* mean?

Look at the picture and read the conversation

Sasha: Let me show you my beautiful kitchen.

Daisey: Oh, it's nice. I like the stove, but there are a lot of dishes in the sink.

Sasha: Yeah, I didn't have time to wash them. I love to cook, but I don't like doing the dishes!

Daisey: Hmm, I hope the glass you gave me was clean.

Sasha: Of course it was! I'm not that bad.

TRUE or FALSE

Daisey likes the stove. _____

Sasha loves washing the dishes. _____

Daisey's glass is dirty. _____

Sasha loves to cook. _____

Would you eat or drink from this kitchen? Why or why not?

DARA SAYS!

- ❖ **Washing** the dishes and **doing** the dishes mean the same thing, to clean the dishes.
- ❖ It's not good to keep dishes in the sink for a long time. It is unsanitary (not clean).

Let's talk about dishes

Dishes are utensils we use to cook and eat food. There are many types of dishes but these are the most common ones.

Which of these utensils are used to <u>cut</u> food?

Fork   Table spoon   Tea spoon   Butter knife

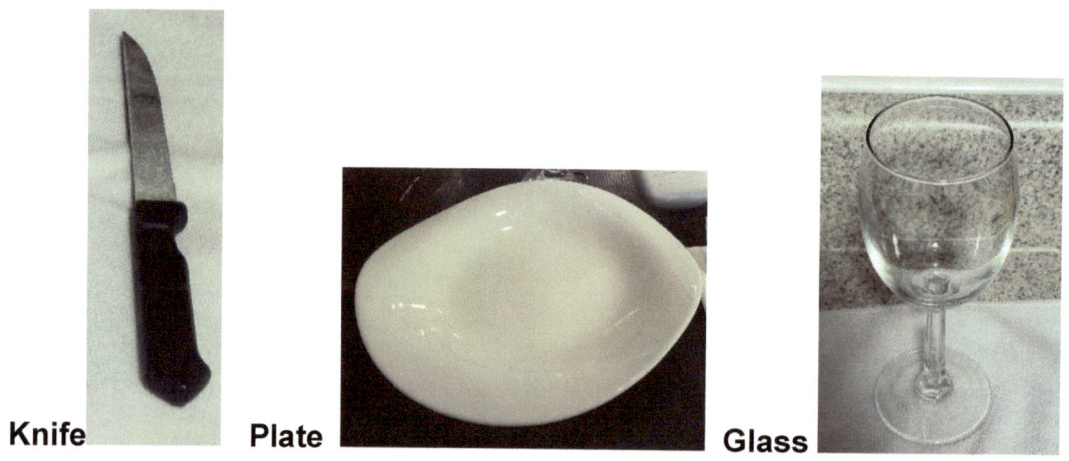

Knife   Plate   Glass

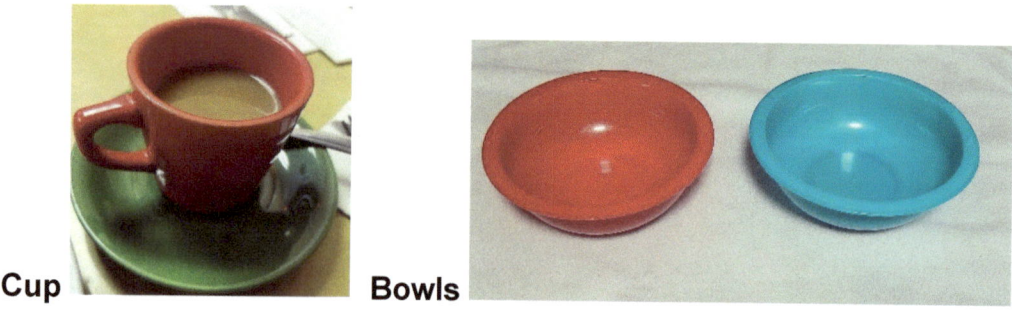

Cup   Bowls

Write the name of the utensil (s) you use for each food dish

Salad

_____

Chicken with noodles and vegetables

_____

Coffee

_____

Mixed fruit

_____

Wine   **Bagels (bread)**

Which of these foods you **DO NOT** need to use an utensil?

A   **B**

Hummus   **Pizza**

Answer: _____

Which of these foods do you like to eat?

DARA SAYS!

- ❖ It is always polite to ask for something in a person's home. For example, *"May I have?"* or *"Where is your bathroom?"*
- ❖ Never do anything that may be uncomfortable to the person in their home.
- ❖ Remember you are the guest (visitor) and the person who invited you is the host.

Let's Cook!

Look at the pictures and answer the questions

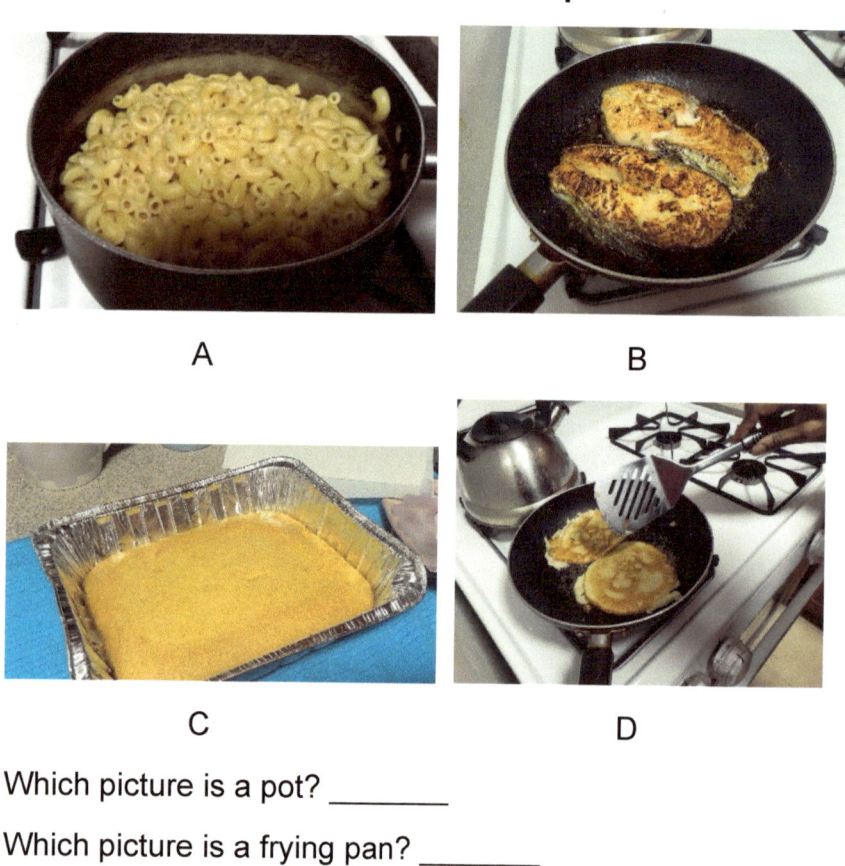

A

B

C

D

Which picture is a pot? _____

Which picture is a frying pan? _____

Which picture is NOT a pot or frying pan? _____

How do we cook food?

We cook food using different types of pots and pans.

Vocabulary

Pot: a round container used to cook food
Frying pan: a flat bottom pot that is used to fry or brown food
Lid: a cover for a pot or pan
Aluminum pan: a round or squared pan that is used to bake food. It is disposable (throw away after use)
Boil: to cook food in water or oil
Fry: to cook food until it turns brown
Steam: to let food cook in water until water evaporates (steam)
Ingredients: food or substances to cook or bake a dish
Spatula: a flat blade, utensil used to mix, spread, or lift food from a frying pan
Whisk: a utensil used to mix food in a bowl
Measuring cup: a cup used to measure ingredients for cooking
Muffin pan (also called cupcake pans): to bake muffins or cupcakes

Matching: match the picture with the correct word

Pot	Aluminum pan	Whisk	Measuring cup	Spatula	Fry	Bake	Boil	Muffin pan

1. _____

2. _____

3. _____

4. _____

5. _____

6. _____

7. _____

8. _____

9. _____

Let's bake a cake

Recipe: a list of ingredients and directions on how to cook something

Read the recipe. Use the recipe to answer the questions from the conversation.

Ingredients you will need:

3 eggs
1 cup of water or milk
1/3 cup of butter
Cake mix
Salt is optional
*****Oil (for pan only)**

1. Put ingredients into a bowl. Use a whisk and stir everything together until everything is mixed well.
2. Use oil to grease the pan so the cake won't stick to the pan while baking
3. Pour cake mix into aluminum pan
4. Turn on oven to 350 degrees
5. Put cake into the oven.

Bake time: 25-35 minutes

When cake is golden brown, take it out of the oven. Use a fork to stick the middle of the cake. It should be clean to know it is done.

Cut the cake and enjoy!

"Hey Lisa, let's bake a cake!"

Anika: I'm hungry, what about you?

Lisa: Me too. I don't know what to eat. Any ideas?

Anika: I know! Let's bake a cake.

Lisa: Sounds good, but I don't know how to make one.

Anika: No problem. I have the recipe, but I don't have an aluminum pan.

Lisa: I'll go to the store and buy one.

Anika: Oh, and don't forget to buy oil.

What does Anika want to eat? _____

What does Anika need to bake the cake? _____

TRUE or FALSE

Anika has all the ingredients for the cake. _____

Lisa doesn't want to go to the store. _____

Lisa: I'm back. Wait! You already started making the cake?

Anika: Relax. I put all the ingredients into the bowl and started stirring it together.

Lisa: Wow, you must be really hungry. So, what are the ingredients?

Anika: Water, butter, a little milk, 3 eggs, and the cake mix.

Lisa: Are you going to put the oil in the cake mix?

Anika: No. The oil is to grease the aluminum pan. That will prevent the cake from sticking.

Lisa: Okay. What can I do to help?

Anika: Turn on the oven to 350 and wait for the cake to rise!

Lisa: When will it be done?

Anika: About 25 to 35 minutes.

TRUE or FALSE

Anika started preparing the cake. _____

Lisa forgot to buy the oil. _____

It will take 25 to 35 minutes to bake the cake. _____

Anika does not have to oil the aluminum pan. _____

Lisa doesn't want to help Anika. _____

Why is it important to check the cake with a fork before taking it out the oven?

DARA SAYS!

- ❖ Always read the recipe carefully. Sometimes, you can add ingredients or make adjustments to a recipe. Always taste your food before continuing. This will avoid mistakes.
- ❖ Pay attention to the oven or stove when cooking. Never leave it unattended. This can cause your food to burn or can cause a fire.
- ❖ Every pot and pan have different purposes. Use the pots you are comfortable using. Some pots can only be used on top of the stove. If you want to use a pot or frying pan in an oven, read the instructions on the back of the pot or pan.
- ❖ Never put the flame too high on the stove. It can burn you.
- ❖ Make sure all your pots and pans are clean before using them. Dirty pans will make your food taste bad and you can get sick.

Supermarket Food Labels and Circulars

What do you buy at the supermarket?

A **supermarket** is a large store that sells food and non-food items such as things for the household and toiletries.

There are different sections to a supermarket: **produce** (fruit and vegetables), **dairy** (milk, yogurt, eggs, and cheese), **meats**, **drinks**, **frozen food**, **snacks**, **canned food**, **seasonings**, **and baked goods** (bread and desserts), **household** (cleaning items), or **toiletries** (soap, toilet tissue, lotion, deodorant), and **pet food**.

What do you buy at a supermarket? Write a list.

1. _____

2. _____

3. _____

4. _____

5. _____

6. _____

7. _____

8. _____

9. _____

10. _____

Vocabulary

Supermarket food labels: a small label or sign that shows the price of a food item
Circular (also called a flyer): an announcement that shows a list of all the food and non-food items that are on sale for the week
Cost: price of something
Buy 1 Get 1 Free: to buy an item and get the same item for free
Expensive: something that costs a lot of money
Cheap: something that doesn't cost a lot of money
More than: something that is a higher amount than something else
Less than: something that is a lower amount than something else

Examples of labels

Read each label and answer the questions

How much is the baby spinach? _____

What food item is expensive? _____

What food item is cheap? _____

What does **2/$7.00** mean? _____

TRUE or FALSE

The cost of the potato chips are **more than** than the water. _____

The cost of fruit punch is **less than** the chicken. _____

The raisin bran cereal is free. _____

Look at the circular and read the conversation. Answer the questions.

Customer: Excuse me, how much are the peppers?

Cashier: They are $1.69 per pound.

Customer: Okay. On the circular it says $1.69 lb. What does lb. mean?

Cashier: Lb. means pound. Would you like to add that to your list?

Customer: Yes, and how much are the cantaloupes?

Cashier: The cantaloupes are on sale today. You can buy 2 for five dollars.

Customer: Great! I will buy them.

Cashier: Anything else?

Customer: Yes, I'll add the bag of oranges for $3.99.

1. What did the customer buy? _____

2. How much is the bag of oranges? _____

3. What is on sale? _____

4. What does *lb* mean? _____

5. What other items are on sale?

_____

What do *you* want to buy? Look at the food labels and its prices. What items do you want to buy and explain why.

Write your answer here

DARA SAYS!

- ❖ Always pay attention to the *sales date* on a circular. Sale prices change weekly.
- ❖ Always pay attention to the *sales price* of an item on a label or circular. Ask the cashier if you are not sure of the price.
- ❖ For food items, pay attention to the *expiration date*. The **expiration date** is the date an item will expire.
- ❖ **Buy 1 Get 1 Free** also means **two for the price of one**. This means that you pay one price for two of the same item. This means the item is on sale

Transportation: How to read bus and train schedules

Vocabulary

Transportation: move from one place to another
Bus: a vehicle that takes people from one place to another
Train: a vehicle that takes people from one place to another on tracks (underground or above ground)
Destination: place or location
Route: direction
Schedule: time
Boulevard (Blvd): a wide street in a city or town
Shuttle buses: take customers to the stops that trains are not going to because of schedule or route changes
Rely: to depend
Inform: to announce, give information
Delay: late
Cancellation: to cancel, to stop
Platform: place to stand when waiting for a train
Catch the bus or catch the train: an idiom that means to take
Apps: applications to download on mobile phones

Weekday bus morning schedule

Kit Avenue	10th Street	Brick Avenue	Day Avenue	15th Street	Madison Avenue
12:20	-----	12:40	12:50	1:00	----
1:20	-----	----	1:50	2:00	----
2:20	-----	2:40	2:50	3:00	3:10
3:20	-----	3:40	3:50	4:00	4:10
4:00	4:10	4:20	4:30	4:45	4:55
5:00	5:10	5:20	5:30	5:45	5:55

5:00 ex	----	-----	5:20	5:30	5:45
6:00	6:10	6:20	6:30	6:45	6:55
6:00 ex	----	----	6:20	6:30	6:45
7:00	7:10	7:20	7:30	7:45	7:55
7:00 ex	7:05	7:10	7:20	7:30	7:45

*ex= express

Read the conversation

A. Good morning, I want to get to <u>15th street</u>. What time should I *catch the bus*?

B. Where are you coming from?

A. I am coming from Kit Avenue.

B. OK. You can take either the express or regular bus to get to 15th street.

A. Okay, thanks.

Answer the question: What time should person A catch the bus?

_____

Read the conversation

C. I need to get to <u>Madison Avenue</u>. What time should I *catch the bus*?

D. When do you need to get there?

C. I need to get there by 2:30.

D. The bus won't arrive to Madison Avenue until 3:10. Where are you coming from?

C. 10th Street.

D. There are no buses arriving at 10th Street until 4:10. So, take the 2:40 bus at Brick Avenue and you will arrive to Madison Avenue at 3:10.

C. Great! Thanks so much.

Answer the questions

1. Where does person C want to go?

_____

2. What time does person C need to get their destination?

_____

3. Where is person C coming from?

_____

4. Can person C take the bus from their location? Why?

_____

5. How can person C get to their final destination?

_____

_____

"Where is my train?" Train announcements

Train announcements are important to inform customers about train delays, <u>cancellations</u>, or service changes. Train delays can cause crowds inside the train and on the <u>platform</u>.

How do *you* feel about train delays?

Read the weekday evening train schedule

Market street	164 street	Beach Avenue	93-96 Boulevard	25 street	Day street	Penny Avenue
5:00	5:04	5:08	5:10	5:20	5:30	5:40
6:10	6:14	6:18	6:20	6:30	6:40	6:50
7:00	7:04	7:08	7:10	7:20	7:30	7:40
8:05	8:09	8:13	8:15	8:25	8:35	8:45
9:00	9:04	9:08	9:10	9:20	9:30	9:40
10:15	10:19	10:23	10:25	10:35	10:45	10:50
11:20	11:25	11:30	11:33	----	----	----
12:01	12:07	12:13	12:17	12:30	----	----
1:05	----	1:18	1:22	1:32	1:42	1:52
2:10	----	2:23	2:25	2:35	2:45	2:55
3:01	3:07	3:13	3:15	3:25	3:35	3:45

*P=peak hours
*OP=off peak hours

Read the announcement:

"There are no trains going to 25 street, Day street and Penny Avenue. Take the shuttle bus at 93-96 Boulevard to get to those stops."

Read the conversation between the train clerk and the customer

Customer: Excuse me, what time is it? I am trying to get to Penny Avenue.
Train clerk: It is now 11:15.
Customer: I am here at 164th street but I can't take this train Penny Avenue. How do I get there?
Train clerk: Take the next train to 93-96 Boulevard and catch the shuttle bus to Penny Avenue.
Customer: Okay, thanks.

Answer the questions

1. What should the customer do to get to Penny Avenue?

2. I took the 12:01 train from Market street. I want to get to Day street. What should I do?

3. I want to go to Penny Avenue from Beach Avenue during off peak hours. Do I need to take the shuttle bus? Why?

DARA SAYS!

- ❖ It is always good to ask a train clerk or someone who works at the train station about <u>schedule</u> changes. They will give you the correct information and help you get to your <u>destination</u>.
- ❖ Don't <u>rely</u> on strangers for correct information.

- ❖ There are transit <u>apps</u> (applications) you can download on your mobile phone to give you alerts on train and bus schedule changes, delays, or re-routes (changes in destination)
- ❖ <u>Shuttle buses</u> take customers to the stops that trains skip because of schedule or route changes.
- ❖ For bus <u>delays</u> or schedule changes, there are usually signs at the bus stop or a bus clerk who will <u>inform</u> customers of bus <u>route</u> changes.

Local Street and Highway Signs

What are street signs?

Street signs are things we see that gives us directions and instructions.

What is the difference between a local street sign and highway signs?

Local Street Signs gives directions on streets that are small, have lower speed limits, and instructions where people can walk, drive, or ride a bicycle.

Highways are high speed roadways that connects cities and towns. They have higher speed limits and more traffic.

Highway signs give directions to drivers or warnings on the highway such as construction and weather warnings.

Examples of local street signs

Stop sign

Pedestrian walk sign

Signal Ahead

No bicycles allowed

Sidewalk closed sign

Speed limit

Dead End

Push to walk

Speed bump sign

Match the sign with the correct meaning

1. To walk _____
2. The sidewalk is closed _____
3. No bicycles _____
4. Traffic must prepare to see the signals (red, yellow, green)
5. To stop _____
6. End of a street or road _____
7. Direction to walk on sidewalk _____
8. Bump to prevent speeding _____
9. Limit of speed _____

a. Stop sign
b. No bicycles allowed
c. Speed bump sign
d. Pedestrian Walk Sign
e. Dead End
f. Sidewalk closed
g. Speed limit
h. Signal Ahead
i. Push button to walk

Construction or Work Ahead signs: signs that direct traffic when there is work on the street or highway. These signs are in orange color.

| 1 | 2 | 3 | 4 |

1. **Slow sign:** to warn drivers to slow down
2. **Flagger:** a construction worker that directs traffic when there is work on the road
3. **Detour:** change in direction
4. **Work zone:** to let drivers know there is construction work ahead

TRUE OR FALSE

1. Teacher Dara can ride a bicycle on the sidewalk

   _____

2. Teacher Dara must walk in a different direction

   _____

Look at the signs and answer the questions

1. How many signs are in the first picture? _____

2. Which picture shows the direction of a place? _____

3. **This sign means there are 3 or more curves ahead**
Choose the correct answer: a. ramp b. winding road ahead c. exit

4. This sign shows 2 highway signs for 2 different locations _____

5. This sign does **NOT** show the exit sign _____

A

B

C

D

6. Which places are **NOT** highways? _____

A

B

C

7. Which sign (s) are *highway* signs? _____

DARA SAYS!

- ❖ Always look both ways when crossing the street. Pay attention to the lights: Green light means to go. Yellow light means to wait. Red light means to stop.
- ❖ **Jaywalking** means when a pedestrian crosses the street without waiting for the walk signal. This is against the law, but many people still jaywalk.
- ❖ Be careful of bicycle lanes. Sometimes **cyclists** (people who ride a bike) don't always follow the right of way rules. Always cross the street with caution.

- ❖ Pay attention to the **speed limit** on the street. The number on a speed limit sign means the amount of speed or **miles per hour (mph)** you can go. **Photo enforced** means if a car goes faster than the speed limit, a photo is taken of the car's license plate. The driver will receive a ticket and pay a fee.
- ❖ Highways are different from place to place. Pay attention to the speed limit on a highway. They will be faster than a local street.
- ❖ Always pay attention to any **construction** or **work ahead** signs. This will prepare you to exit the highway or a **flagger** will direct traffic.

Doctor verses Hospital Appointments

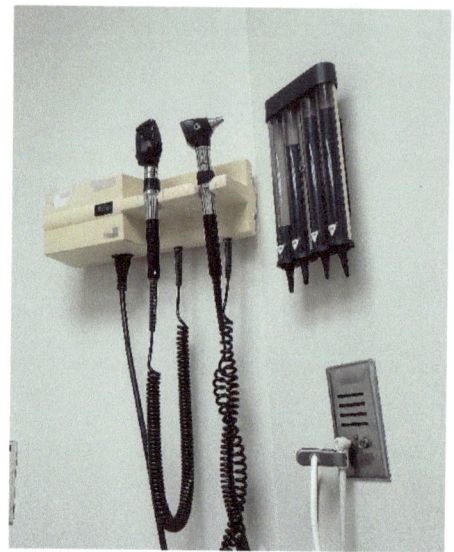 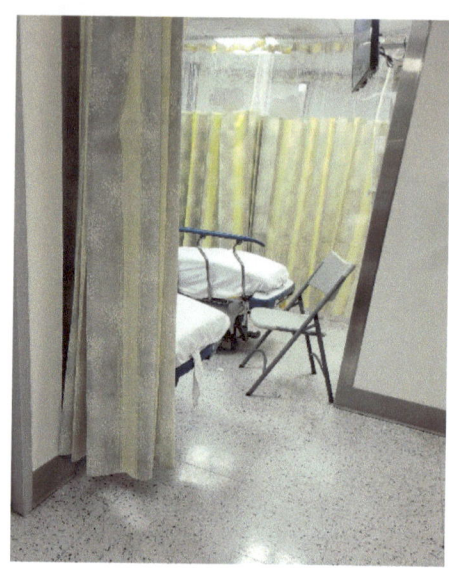

<u>Vocabulary</u>

Doctor/physician- a person who examines a patient and writes prescriptions for patients

Patient- a person who visits and receives treatment from a doctor

Appointment- to schedule a time to see the doctor at a doctor's office or hospital

Receptionist- a person who greets patients and schedule appointments

Walk-in- to walk into a clinic without an appointment

Insurance card- a card that states your health insurance; coverage for healthcare and medicine costs

Co-pay- a certain amount of money the patient must pay for a doctor's visit. The health insurance may cover all or some of the medical fees.

Referral- to refer, to send someone to a place for an exam or treatment

Sick- to feel not well; ill

X-ray- an electromagnetic radiation light that can see through parts of the body

Symptoms- feelings of sickness

Fever- to have high temperature; to feel hot and cold

Sore throat- the throat feels irritated, uncomfortable to speak

Cold- to feel sick due to temperature changes in weather

Let's make a doctor's appointment

Read the conversation and answer the questions

Receptionist: Hello, doctor's office.
Patient: Hi, I would like to make an appointment to see the doctor.
Receptionist: What is the problem?
Patient: I feel sick. My head hurts a lot and I feel hot all the time.
Receptionist: When did this start?
Patient: One week ago.
Receptionist: Okay. Can you come in tomorrow at 9 am?
Patient: Yes.
Receptionist: Do you have insurance?
Patient: No, I don't.
Receptionist: Okay, you will have to pay a fee of $75.00 after your appointment. We take cash, debit, or credit card.
Patient: Okay, no problem.
Receptionist: Great. So, we will see you tomorrow at 9 am. Thank you and have a good day.
Patient: Thank you.

1. What is wrong with the patient?

2. How long did the patient have this problem?

3. When will the patient go to the doctor's office?

4. Does the patient have insurance?

5. What much does it cost to see the doctor?

Let's make a hospital appointment

Read the conversation and answer the questions

Receptionist: Hello, how may I help you?
Patient: Hi, I would like to make an appointment to see the doctor.
Receptionist: Which doctor would you like to see?
Patient: My doctor referred me to this hospital to get an X-ray.
Receptionist: What is your doctor's name?
Patient: Doctor Julie West.
Receptionist: Okay. We have 3 appointments available. One at 11am, 2pm, and 3pm. Which one works for you?
Patient: Can I come in at 2pm?
Receptionist: Okay, I will *put you down* for 2pm. Please bring your insurance card, and referral from your doctor. Don't wear any metal jewelry.
Patient: Okay.
Receptionist: Is there anything else I can help you with?
Patient: No. Thanks so much.
Receptionist: Have a good day, bye bye.
Patient: Bye.

*__Put you down__ means to add you to something like a schedule or an appointment.

1. Why is the patient making an appointment to the hospital?

2. What kind of exam does the patient need?

3. Why can't the patient wear metal jewelry?

4. Who referred the patient to go to the hospital?

What is the difference between a doctor's office and a hospital?

Appointments at both places will be different for each patient. Some appointments will be short and some will last a long time. This will depend on how many patients are waiting to see the doctor. At a hospital, there are many doctors and exams. Every patient will have a different kind of appointment at a hospital. A hospital is very busy. It is important to keep your appointment or reschedule. For exams, like an X-ray, it's very important to follow the instructions of the hospital or the doctor.

Where do you go to see the doctor? Why? _____

_____

_____

Read the health insurance card and answer the questions

ABC Health Insurance

Steven Joseph   **DOB:** 3/19/1979
Patient ID number: 1586LWX
Doctor's name: Dr. Joy Heart
Doctor's phone: (123) 456-7890
Visit co-pay: $35.00

What is the name of the health insurance?

_____

What is the patient's name?

_____

What is the patient's date of birth?

_____

What is the co-pay?

_____

What is the doctor's name?

_____

Read the conversation between the patient and the doctor

Doctor: Hello, how are you feeling today?
Patient: Not too good doctor.
Doctor: What is the problem?
Patient: I feel hot all the time and my head hurts.
Doctor: Do you take medicine for this?
Patient: Yes, I take aspirin but I still feel the same.
Doctor: And how long did you have these symptoms?
Patient: For one week.
Doctor: Okay. Let me check your throat. Open wide and say "ahh"
Patient: Ahh…
Doctor: Hmm…your throat looks red. Let me take your temperature.
Patient: Okay.
Doctor: Your temperature is 103 degrees. Your throat is red and you said your head hurts. It sounds like you have a bad cold.
Patient: Okay, what can I do?
Doctor: Well, I would continue to take aspirin, drink plenty of fluids, and rest. If you don't improve in a couple of days, please come back here. If you start to feel worse, go to the hospital immediately, okay?
Patient: Okay.

TRUE or FALSE

1. The patient feels sick. _____

2. The doctor told the patient to take aspirin, rest, and go to the hospital.

_____

3. The patient had symptoms for two weeks. _____

4. The doctor checked the patient's temperature and throat. _____

5. The patient does not have a cold. _____

6. The patient's temperature is 103 degrees. _____

DARA SAYS!

- ❖ The way you make a doctor's appointment or hospital appointment will vary depending on the country.
- ❖ Some doctor's appointments are not done over the phone and instead done in person.
- ❖ There are different ways to see the doctor: **walk in** (walk into a clinic without an appointment), an **appointment** (a scheduled time for a person to see the doctor).
- ❖ **Urgent care:** some clinics will have an urgent care center for emergencies. No appointments are necessary
- ❖ Not all clinics will accept health insurance or do not have health insurance
- ❖ **Pay-out-of-pocket:** to pay for doctor services, a fee
- ❖ **Always ask questions if you are not sure about a clinic's policies**

Public Restrooms

A **public restroom** is a place to use the bathoom for public use. Public restrooms are found in public places like stores, restaurants, parks, and hospitals. Public restrooms have **stalls**; a place for people to use the bathroom privately. Restroom and bathroom have the same meaning.

Do you go to a public restroom? Where do you go to use a public restroom?

Read the conversation and answer the questions

Amir: Rob, do you want to go to the park?
Rob: Yeah man, let's go to Bay Park. It has a huge lake with ducks!
Amir: That's cool, but I have to go to the bathroom. Are there any restrooms close by?
Rob: Yes, there are public restrooms in the park.
Amir: Phew, that's great. Okay, let's go.

1. Where are Amir and Rob going?

2. What did Amir ask Rob?

3. TRUE or FALSE: There are no public restrooms in the park.

What is inside a public restroom?

   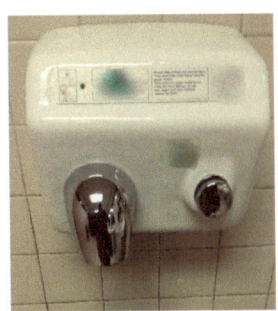

Toliet   **Sink**   **Automated soap dispenser** **Hand dryer**

Toliet: a basin to relieve yourself

Sink: to wash your hands

Automated sink dispenser: a machine that releases liquid soap

Hand dryer: a machine to air dry hands

Hand dryer with tissue: put hand in front of dryer to automatically release tissue

Rail and HELP button: The rail helps people who have a difficult time with their balance.

HELP button or string: to alert a medical

staff member in an emergency. It is common in hospitals and doctor's offices

Which hand dryer do you prefer? _____

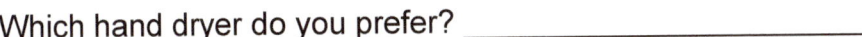

"Knock knock…is anyone in there?"

<u>**Read the conversations and answer the questions**</u>

A. Hello? Is anyone in there?
B. Yes.
A. Okay. I'm sorry.

<u>**Conversation 2**</u>

A. Hey, is everything okay in there?
B. I need help.
A. Okay, let me get a nurse.
Nurse: Hello, can you open the door?
A. The door is open.
Nurse: Let me help you off the floor.
A. Thank you. I feel so embarrassed.
Nurse: Don't be, it happens sometimes. Are you hurt?
A. My arm hurts.
Nurse: Okay, let me take you to a doctor.
A. Thank you.

1. What is the difference between conversation 1 and 2?

2. Why did the nurse come into the bathroom stall?

3. Why is it important to knock on the stall?

DARA SAYS!

- ❖ Some public restrooms have many stalls, but some only have one stall.
- ❖ Always lock the stall or door.
- ❖ If someone knocks on the door, say "yes" or "someone is in here" so the person knows not to keep knocking (some people will keep knocking or try to open the locked door).
- ❖ To say "one second" or "one minute" it means to wait.
- ❖ NEVER sit on the toilet directly. Squat or put tissue on the toilet seat to sit on it.
- ❖ Always wash your hands.

What kind of job do you want?

Name the job or jobs you would like to have

1. _____

2. _____

3. _____

4. _____

5. _____

Why do you want these jobs? (There are no right or wrong answers)

What is a job?

A job means work or a task.

What is the different between a *job* and *employment*?

Employment means a **paid** job, to be employed or hired.

What is the difference between a job and a career?

A **career** means a job that is long-term in a person's life

Job versus Career

Complete the chart of job and career

Job	Career
Store cashier	Store owner
Office assistant	Office director
Computer repair person	Computer technician specialist

What careers are you interested in? Why?

_____

_____

_____

How to find a job or a career?

Job Search: to look for a job (work, employment)

Ways to find a job?

- Internet (www.)
- Newspaper job advertisements (ads)
- Employment agencies or walk in
- Networking
- Word-of-mouth, referral

The internet is an easy and great way to look for jobs. It takes time but there are many opportunities available. This includes remote work-hybrid work.

Remote work-Hybrid work: Remote work means to work at home. Hybrid work means to work from home on some days and to work at a workplace on other days.

Teacher Dara is working from home

Read the job ad and answer the questions

Temporary Work /Administrative Assisant

Short Term and Long Term
• Providing full administrative support

• Manage Travel & Expense
• Calendar management
• Handle phones calls
• Coordinate meetings   in person
• Assist in producing presentations
• Maintaining various files
• Interact with individuals at all levels of an organization
• Handle multiple high priority tasks, muti task

• Assist in   meetings, and events
• Maintain office files, records

1. Would you apply for this job? Why or why not?

_____

_____

2. What do you like about this job position?

_____

_____

3. What do you dislike about this job position?

_____

_____

4. Do you feel you qualify for this job position? Why?

_____

_____

Newspaper job advertisements (also called Classified Ads or Help Wanted): short job postings that state the job position (name of job) type of job (full time, part time), location, requirements needed (skills, education, job experience), contact information, company name (sometimes).

Example of Classified Ads

Read the job ad. Answer the questions

What are the **job positions**?

_____

How much is the pay *after* training?

_____

How do you **apply** for the jobs?

_____

TRUE or FALSE

Both of these jobs are the same. _____

Bilingual means to speak 2 languages. _____

Job ads use *abbreviations*. **Abbreviations** are short ways of writing words.
For example: Full time= F/T (abbreviation)

Match the word with its abbreviation

a. Part-time   _____ res
b. Requirements   _____ exp
c. Experience   _____ P/T
d. Resume   _____ req

Employment agencies: places that help people find jobs.

People who work at employment agencies are called **job developers** or **career advisors**. They help people in their job search, how to apply for work, interview skills and resume writing.

People who look for work are **job applicants**, **customers**, or **clients**.

 Which would you prefer, **remote, hybrid,** or **in person** work? Why?

What skills do you need to apply for a job or career?

A **skill** is something you know how to do. The skills you need to apply for a job or a career will depend on the type of job or career you want.

If you are not sure what it takes to apply for the job or career you want, you can use *transferrable skills*.

Transferrable skills: the skills you have that can be used towards a job or career.

Example of transferrable skills:
Communication (languages)
Typing
Answering phones
Writing
Helping people
Teaching
Organizing

Management and multi-tasking (at work or at home, example: taking care of family)

What are *your* **transferrable skills**?

1. _____

2. _____

3. _____

4. _____

5. _____

Temporary Work /Administrative Assisant

Short Term and Long Term
- Providing full administrative support

- Manage Travel & Expense
- Calendar management
- Handle phones calls
- Coordinate meetings.   in person
- Assist in producing presentations
- Maintaining various files
- Interact with individuals at all levels of an organization
- Handle multiple high priority tasks, muti task

- Assist in   meetings, and events
- Maintain office files, records

What transferrable skills do you have to apply for this job?

_____

_____

Dara Says! Tips

- ❖ Take your time when looking for a job. Use job search websites, newspapers, job agencies, or **job apps (applications)** to help you.

- ❖ Network with people you know. Ask them to assist you in your job search. They may know of job openings at their workplaces.

- ❖ For remote jobs, always check to make sure the job is 100% remote. Some job ads won't specify if the job is remote only or hybrid, so contact the employer to check.

- ❖ A career is a long-term type of employment, so choose a job that you can see yourself working at for years.

- ❖ Make sure your resume is **up-to-date (current)** and include your transferrable skills

Let's go Shopping!

"I want a refund!" Read the conversation.

Scott: I want to *exchange* this shirt for a pair of pants.

Customer service representative: Okay, do you have a *receipt*?

Scott: No, I don't. I was just here yesterday.

Customer service representative: I'm sorry, I can't exchange an item without a receipt.

Scott: Really? Fine! I want a *refund*.

Customer service representative: I would still need to see a receipt for an exchange or a refund. This is the *store policy*.

Scott: Are you serious? I don't want this shirt! Give me my money now!

Vocabulary

Refund: to get money back from a purchase (something you bought)
Exchange: to change an item for another one
Receipt: a record of all the things you bought
Store policy: the rules of the store
Customer: a person that buys something
Customer service representative: a person that helps and answers customers' questions

 Do you think the customer should get a refund? Why?

What's your size?

There are different sizes for clothes: shirt, pants, shorts, skirt, dress, jeans, coat, and jacket

XS= extra small

S= small

M= medium

L= large

XL= extra large

2XL-5XL= plus sizes (larger sizes)

*These are based on American clothing sizes. Some clothes can be in <u>number size</u>. For example, "I wear a **size 18** in pants." This means the person wears an **extra-large (XL)** in pants.

Shoe sizes are in numbers based on a person's foot size. Example: "I wear a size 6," or "My shoe size is 6."

What is your size? _____

What is your shoe size? _____

What is your favorite clothing? Circle your answers.

a. pants   b. shirt   c. skirt   d. dress   e. shoes   f. sneakers   g. coat   h. jacket

What is Teacher Dara wearing? Write what she is wearing under each picture

_____

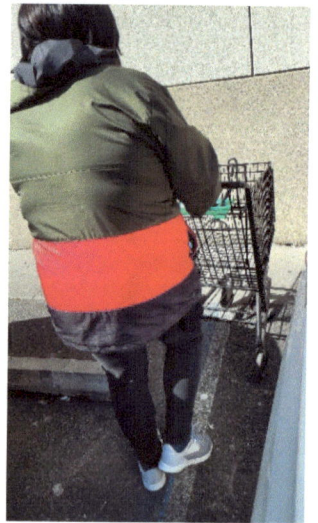

_____

_____

Read the ad

SALE

Men's shirts are 50% off its original price
Women's dresses are 50% off its original price
Free pair of pants with a purchase of $100 or more
Women's jackets are 10% off its original price

Sale ends May 1st. No exchanges or refunds after end of sale date

Answer the questions:

What clothes are on sale?

_____

When does the sale end? _____

What can you get for free? _____

Can you get an exchange or a refund? _____

Read the conversation between the customer and salesperson

Customer: Excuse me. I am looking for a shirt.

Salesperson: Okay, what size shirt?

Customer: I need a 2XL.

Salesperson: Okay, I will show you our 2XL shirts. Come with me.

Customer: Thank you.

Answer the question: What size shirt does the customer want?

_____

Read the conversation

Customer: Excuse me. I need a pair of women's <u>shoes</u>.

Salesperson: What size do you wear?

Customer: Size 8.

Salesperson: Oh, we don't have any more size 8. We only have size 10.

Customer: Okay. I would like a pair of <u>sneakers</u>. Do you have women's size 8 ½ ?

Salesperson: Let me check. Yes, we have a size 8 ½ in women's sneakers. What color would you like?

Customer: Black.

Salesperson: Okay, let me get you a pair to *try on*. One second.

Customer: Okay, thank you.

Answer the questions: What size shoes and sneakers do the customer want?

_____

Why can't the customer get shoes in a size 8?

_____

DARA SAYS!

- ❖ Always pay attention to the sale ad. Sales always have an end date and information about the sales prices, refunds or exchanges.
- ❖ When you ask about shoe sizes, we say, "I would like a size ___ in shoes," or " I wear a size ___ "
- ❖ A **pair of shoes** means two shoes. Pair means two. We DO NOT say, *"I want a shoe"* because we have 2 feet (feet is plural for foot), and we wear two shoes. We also say the same thing for pants: I want a *pair of pants*.
- ❖ If you want to buy more than one "shoe," you will say, *"I want to buy **two pairs of shoes.**"* This means the number of shoes you want to buy.
- ❖ **Try on** is an idiom meaning to try something on your body. For example, "I want to *try on* the shoes, or I want to *try on* the shirt."
- ❖ Always try on shoes before buying them. Every shoe fits differently for every shoe size. You always want to try on the shoes and walk in them before buying. If not, then you will have shoes you cannot wear.

Going Out to Eat

Let's look at the different food places to eat

Restaurant

Food cart (also known as food truck)

Pizza shop

Bakery

Differences between a restaurant and other food places

- **Restaurants** are the most common places to eat. You can find a variety of food and drinks ranging in culture, taste, and style. A <u>waiter</u> or <u>waitress</u> (also called servers) takes customers' orders and serves them their food. Every restaurant is different and can range in size, food type, casual or fancy atmosphere, and costs (cheap or expensive).

- **Food carts, hot dog stands, pizza shops, and take out restaurants** are considered "fast food restaurants," because the food is prepared fast and you receive your food quickly. There are no servers. These places are cheaper than restaurants and diners.

- **Bakeries**, similar to cafes, serve fresh baked food. Usually there is a sign that says, "All baked goods are done on the premises," meaning all food is prepared at the bakery. Some bakeries serve coffee and tea. Bakeries can be a **sit-in** (sit inside the bakery) or **take out** (order-to-go).

How to order food from a restaurant versus a food cart

RESTAURANT-Read the conversation between the server and the customer

Server: Hi there, what can I get you?

Customer: Hi, I would like the chicken and rice dish.

Server: Sure. Do you want that with a salad?

Customer: Yes please, and can I get a glass of wine.

Server: Sure, would you like anything else?

Customer: No, that's all.

Server: Okay, I'll get that to you in a bit.

FOOD CART-Read the conversation between the customer and server

Customer: Good morning. Can I get a large coffee light and sweet?

Food cart server: Sure, anything else?

Customer: Lemme get a bagel with butter.

Food cart server: Do you want it toasted?

Customer: Yeah.

Lemme is informal for let me

Answer the questions

1. What did the customer order from the restaurant?

2. What did the customer order from the coffee cart?

3. What is the difference between a restaurant and a coffee cart?

4. Where do you like to eat? Why?

You Try: Write a conversation between a customer and a server. You can choose between a restaurant, food cart, pizza shop, or bakery.

Server: Hi, what can I get you?

You: I would like

Server:

You:

Server:

You:

Server:

You:

DARA SAYS!

- ❖ It is polite to say, "I would like" or "I'd like" or "May I have" when ordering food.
- ❖ Always be polite to the waiter/server. They are there to serve you. Never be rude.
- ❖ If you have any food allergies, let the server know immediately.
- ❖ **"No substitutions please"** means you cannot substitute one item for another. For example, if eggs come with potatoes or toast, you cannot substitute the potatoes or toast with pancakes.

- ❖ Always ask questions if you are not sure about your order
- ❖ Pay for your order. Never leave without paying.
- ❖ **Gratuity** means to give a tip (extra money) to your server for offering exceptional service. Many restaurants have gratuity included in the order. For cafes or smaller food places, gratuity is not included and the customer can choose to tip or not.
  - ➢ In many countries, servers do not request or accept gratuity.

- ❖ Ordering food from a food cart is **fast-paced**. This means you want to be ready to order.
- ❖ Always have your money ready to pay. You can ask *how much?* or the server will tell you the cost of your order.
- ❖ Rarely a **debit** or **credit card** is used to pay at a food cart. If that is an **option**, have your card ready to pay for your order.
- ❖ Sometimes there is a line of people waiting to order their food, or they are waiting for their order. It is polite to step aside after you order your food, and wait for the server to call you. They may say your order or point to you.
- ❖ Informal English is common when placing an order at a food cart. Always be polite.

APPENDIX A

Grammar points

Parts of Speech

Noun: people, places, things, animals, or an idea
Pronoun: replaces a noun
Example: I, me, you, we, us, they, them, he, his, she, her, it
Possessive pronouns (use to show ownership): my, his, her, our, their, theirs, your, yours
Example: My book. Her book. Your book. Their book. Our book.
Verb: an action word
Example: talk, listen, dance, watch, play
Adjective: a word that describes a noun
Example: beautiful, ugly, big, small, tall, short
Adverb: a word or phrase that describes, modifies, or quantifies an adjective, verb, or adverb. It can also express time, place, or a circumstance
*Most adverbs end in -ly
Example: really, randomly, abruptly, financially, quickly
For time (when and where something happened) or circumstances: here, often, there, everywhere, outside, inside, now, today, tomorrow, later
Preposition: connects a noun to another word
Example: at, after, to, on, but
Conjunction: joins sentences, words, or clauses together
Example: and, but, when
Example sentences: **When** I go to the doctor, I feel better.
We bought two shirts, three ties, **and** one coat.
He wants to go to school, **but** he doesn't feel well.

The is a <u>definite article</u> to talk about something specific. It is used before a noun
Interjection: short words or words with exclamation that are sometimes put in a sentence.
Example: Hi! Ouch! Oh! Well
Example sentence: Ouch! That hurts.

BE VERBS [am, is, are]

<u>BE verbs</u> are verbs that describe an action from people or things.

Subject + BE verb

I	**am**
You	**are**
We	**are**
They	**are**
He	**is**
She	**is**
It	**is**

Example: I am happy. He is hungry. We are tired.

Contractions

I am	**I'm**
You are	**You're**
We are	**We're**
They are	**They're**
He is	**He's**
She is	**She's**
It is	**It's**

(') is called an apostrophe
Use an apostrophe (') to make a contraction.

Negative:
Use *not* to make things negative
Example: I am *not* happy. We are *not* hungry. She is *not* tired.

Simple Present Tense and verbs in the third person (-s, -es, -ies)

We use the present tense when talking about things happening now.

Verb: talk

I	talk
You	talk
We	talk
They	talk
He	talks
She	talks
It	talks

With most verbs, we use **–s** when talking in the third person (he, she, it)
Example: Eat
He eat**s**, She eat**s**, It eat**s**

Verbs that have the following sounds: **s, z, ch, sh, x**, add **–es**
Example: Kis**s**= kisses
He kiss**es**, She kiss**es**, It kiss**es**

Buzz=buz**z**es
He buzz**es**, She buzz**es**, It buzz**es**

Tea**ch**=teaches
He teach**es**, She teach**es**, It teach**es**

Fini**sh**= finishes
He finish**es**, She finish**es**, It finish**es**

Fix= fi**x**es
He fix**es**, She fix**es**, It fix**es**

Verbs that end in **–y** can also change to **–s** when it ends in one *vowel* + y
Example: play
"a" is a vowel
Play= plays
He plays, She plays, It plays

Verbs that end in **–y** can change into **–ies** if it ends with a *consonant* + y
Example: cry
"r" is a consonant
Cry= cries
He cr**ies**, she cr**ies**, it cr**ies**

Irregular verbs: verbs that do not follow the same rules as regular verbs.

Present	Past
go, goes	went
do, does	did
be	was, were
see	saw
eat	ate
become	became
feel	felt
fall	fell
break	broke
come	came
hurt	hurt
choose	chose
cut	cut
have, has	had
know	knew
lay	laid
give	gave
get	got
forgive	forgave
begin	began
drink	drank
bring	brought
make	made
read	read
let	let
lie	lay
hear	heard
meet	met
leave	left
run	ran
pay	paid
quit	quit
sell	sold
send	sent
sit	sat
ride	rode
fight	fought
teach	taught
steal	stole
understand	understood
think	thought
write	wrote
take	took
spend	spent

sleep	slept
speak	spoke

Vowels: a, e, i, o, u and sometimes y
Consonants: all letters except vowels. Y is also a consonant

BE VERBS in the Past Tense [was, were]

<u>BE verbs</u> in the past tense are verbs that describe an action from people or things in the past.

Subject + BE verb

I	**was**
You	**were**
We	**were**
They	**were**
He	**was**
She	**was**
It	**was**

Example: I was happy. He was hungry. We were tired.

Negative

Use *not* to make things negative. Use *not* after the verb.

Example: I was *not* happy.
We were *not* hungry.
She was *not* tired.

Simple Past Tense
We use the past tense when talking about things that happened in the past.

Verb: talk
Add **–ed** to the end of verbs for the past tense

I	talked
You	talked
We	talked
They	talked
He	talked
She	talked
It	talked

Verbs ending in **-e** (the –e is silent), add **–d**
Example: phone= phone**d**
*I phoned my friend. (British English)
I called my friend. (American English)

Close= close**d**
They closed the book.

Verbs ending in a *vowel*+ y, add **-ed**
Example: play= play**ed**
We played the game.

Verbs ending in a consonant+ y, add **-ied**
Example: marry= marr**ied**
She married her boyfriend.

Present Continuous
Present continuous is when something is happening now.

Subject + BE verb (am, is, are) + verb + -ing

Example: listen
I + am + listening.

Example: try
She + is + trying.

*Verb does not change in the third person.

Example: read
You + are + reading.

*Example: go
We use *going* with a noun (place) or verb (action)

I + am + going + to + <u>the supermarket</u>. (noun)

*to is a preposition that connects with the <u>noun</u>

They + are + going + <u>to listen</u>. (verb)

*Example: do
We + are + doing + <u>work</u>
We use *doing* with a <u>noun</u>

Negative
Use *not* to make things negative. Use *not* after the verb.

Example: I am *not* listening.
She is *not* trying.
You are *not* reading.
I am *not* going to the supermarket.
We are *not* doing work.

Past Continuous
Past continuous is when something is happening in the past.

Subject + BE verb (was, were) + verb + -ing

Example: speak
They + were + speaking.

Example: teach
I + was + teaching.

*Example: go
He + was+ going + <u>to the bedroom.</u> (place)
I + was + going <u>+ to think</u> (action)
When we use *going*, we include a verb (an action) or a noun (place)

*Example: do
They + were + doing + <u>homework.</u> (noun)
She + was + doing + <u>laundry.</u>
When we use *doing*, we include a <u>noun</u>

Negative
Use *not* to make things negative. Use *not* after the verb.

Example: There were not speaking.
I was not teaching.
He was not going to the bedroom.
I was not going to think.

Future tense

We use the future tense when talking about something in the future (something that did not happen yet).
We use **will** and **be going to** for the future tense.

We do not change the verb when using **will** or **be going to**

subject + will + verb (no change)

Example: study
I + will + study.

Example: travel
They + will + travel

Example: watch
He + will + watch *TV*.

*Sometimes we can add a *noun* at the end of the sentence

Negative

Use **not** to make things negative. Use **not** after will.

Example: I will **not** study.
They will **not** travel.
He will **not** watch TV.

subject + be going to + verb (no change)

Example: see
We + are going to + see + <u>a movie</u>. (noun)

Example: listen
I + am going to + listen + <u>to music</u>.

Example: read
He + is going to + read+ <u>a book</u>.

When using **be going to**, we can add a noun at the end of a sentence

Negative

Use *not* to make things negative. Use **not** after the BE verb.

Example: We are **not** going to see a movie.
I am **not** going to listen to music.
He is **not** going to read a book.

Present Perfect Tense

We use the present perfect tense to talk about an event that happened in the past but the result is in the present.

Subject + have/has + past participle

Example: I *have* __been__ to New York.
This means you went to New York sometime in the past.

Example: She *has* __talked__ to her friend.
This means she talked to her friend sometime in the past.

Negative

Use *not* to make things negative. Use **not** after have or has

Example: I have **not** been to New York.
She has **not** talked to her friend.

Subject	Have/ has	Past participle
I	have	These verbs have the –ed ending or are irregular
We	have	
You	have	
They	have	
He	has	
She	has	
It	has	

*Some verbs in past participle will be same in present and/or past tense

These are just a few examples of verbs in the past participle

Verb	Past Participle
talk	talked
listen	listened
walk	walked
study	studied
play	played
read	read
hurt	hurt
let	let
run	run
quit	quit
go	gone
be	been
do	done
see	seen

eat	eaten
become	become
begin	begun
give	given
choose	chosen
feel	felt
lay	laid
say	said
speak	spoken
pay	paid
take	taken
sell	sold
understand	understood
write	written
think	thought
teach	taught
sit	sat

We can include **time** *(since, for)* when talking in the present perfect

Subject + have/has + past participle + time

Since is used to state a specific time

I *have* <u>watched</u> the show *since* 10 o'clock.
He *has* <u>taught</u> class *since* yesterday.

For is used to state time (not specific)

We *have* <u>lived</u> in the United States *for* 12 years.
It *has* <u>been</u> raining *for* 3 days.

Negative
I have **not** watched the show *since* 10 o'clock.
He has **not** taught class *since* yesterday.
We have **not** lived in the United States *for* 12 years.
It has **not** been raining *for* 3 days.

'Wh' Questions

What- to ask about information
Example: What is your name?

When- to ask about time (time, day, week, month, year)
Example: When is the doctor's appointment?

Who- to ask about a person or people
Example: Who is the teacher?

Where- to ask about place
Example: Where is the restaurant?

Why- to ask about a reason
Example: Why are you applying for a job?

Which- to compare, to choose
Example: Which shirt do you want to buy?

Yes/ No Questions

Be verb (Am, Is, Are...?)

Example: **Am** I a teacher?
Answer: Yes you **are**. No, you **are not** (No you **aren't**)

Are you a student?
Yes I **am**. No, I **am not** (No, **I'm not**)

Is he a student?
Yes he **is**. No, he **is not**. (No, **he's not** *or* No, he **isn't**)

Is she a student?
Yes she **is**. No, she **is not**. (No, **she's not** *or* No, she **isn't**)

Do or Does...?

I	**do**
You	**do**
We	**do**
They	**do**
He	**does**
She	**does**
It	**does**

Example: **Do** you go to school?

Answer: Yes I **do**. No, I **do not** or No, I **don't**.

Does she go to school?
Yes she **does**. No, she **does not** or No, she **doesn't**.

Will...?

I	will
You	will
We	will
They	will
He	will
She	will
It	will

Example: **Will** you find a job?
Answer: Yes I **will**. No, I **will not** or No, I **won't**.

Will he find a job?
Yes he **will**. No, he **will not** or No, he **won't**.

Will they find a job?
Yes they **will**. No, they **will not** or No, they **won't**.

Will not= won't (contraction)

Modals

Modals are words that express permission, ability, obligation, possibility, advice, probability, prohibition (warning/cannot do something), lack of necessity (not a must)

Modal	Meaning
Can	Ability, permission, possibility
Could	Possibility, permission (polite), ability in the past
May	Permission, possibility, probability
Might	Permission (polite), possibility, probability
Will	Possibility (future)
Would	Permission (polite), possibility
Should, ought to	Advice, some obligation, conclusion
Shall	Make offers, suggestions, advice
Had better	advice
Must	Strong obligation, certainty
Must not	Prohibition
Need not	Lack of necessity/no obligation

We use *can*, *could*, *may*, *will*, *would*, and *shall* when asking questions.

Example: Can you help me?
Could you help me? (polite, more formal)
May I take your order? (polite, formal)
Will you go to the interview?
Would you like to buy the dress?
Shall we take the bus?

APPENDIX B
Vocabulary word definitions

Alphabet: English letters
Numbers: use to count things
Calendar: shows the month, year, days of the week, and dates
Season: different types of weather in a year
Weather: how the day feels (hot, cold, wet, or dry) and the temperature of the day
Temperature: the measure of hot or cold that is expressed in degrees Fahrenheit or Celsius
Holidays: special occasions we celebrate during the year
Time: the hours and minutes in a day
Greetings: to greet, to say hello to someone
Formal: polite way of talking to someone you do not know, or someone who is in authority
Informal: a free, relaxed way of talking to someone you know
Conversation: two or more people talking to each other
Slang: informal English but more informal by the way we say words, expressions, and their meanings
New York City: a city in New York state in the United States
Body language: to communicate using your body (gestures) without speaking
Expressions: words or phrases to relay an idea
What's up with you?- How are you or Are you okay?
I got you: I am here for you
You frontin': You are trying to impress others, not being honest
Don't sleep: to pay attention
Nah, I'm good: No, I'm fine
You feel me?: Do you understand me or Do you believe me?
Sis/Girl/Bro/Hommie: friend
My G: close friend
House: a place you buy to own
Apartment: a place to live
Entrance: the door to enter inside a place
Living room: a place to relax, eat, or watch TV
TV (television): something to watch shows or movies
Kitchen: a place to cook food
Refrigerator: an appliance to keep food cold
Table: a place to sit at
Chair: a seat with four legs to sit on
Bathroom: a place to relieve yourself, wash
Toilet: use to relieve yourself
Bedroom: a place to rest or sleep
Bed: to sleep
I'll be right back: to return, to come back soon
Dishes: utensils used to cook and eat food
Fork: a utensil to pick up food

Spoon: a utensil to scoop up food

Tea spoon: a small spoon

Table spoon: a big spoon

Knife: a utensil to cut food

Butter knife: a knife that is not very sharp

Cup or Glass: to pour liquid in to drink (example: coffee)

Plate: a flat surface to put food on

Wash the dishes/Do the dishes: to clean the dishes

Pot: a round container used to cook food

Frying pan: a flat bottom pot that is used to fry or brown food

Lid: a cover for a pot or pan

Aluminum pan: a round or squared pan that is used to bake food. It is disposable (throw away after use)

Boil: to cook food in water or oil

Fry: to cook food until it turns brown

Steam: to let food cook in water until water evaporates (steam)

Ingredients: food or substances to cook or bake a dish

Spatula: a flat blade, utensil used to mix, spread, or lift food from a frying pan

Whisk: a utensil used to mix food in a bowl

Measuring cup: a cup used to measure ingredients for cooking

Muffin pan (also called cupcake pans): to bake muffins or cupcakes

Recipe: a list of ingredients and directions on how to cook something

Supermarket: a large store that sells food and non-food items such as things for the household and toiletries

Supermarket food labels: a small label or sign that shows the price of a food item

Circular (also called a flyer): an announcement that shows a list of all the food and non-food items that are on sale for the week

Cost: price of something

Buy 1 Get 1 Free/ two for the price of one: to buy an item and get the same item for free; the item is on sale

Expensive: something that costs a lot of money

Cheap: something that doesn't cost a lot of money

More than: something that is a higher amount than something else

Less than: something that is a lower amount than something else

Expiration date: the date the item will expire

Transportation: move from one place to another

Bus: a vehicle that takes people from one place to another

Train: a vehicle that takes people from one place to another on tracks (underground or above ground)

Destination: place or location

Route: direction

Schedule: time

Boulevard (Blvd): a wide street in a city or town

Shuttle buses: take customers to the stops that trains are not going to because of schedule or route changes

Rely: to depend

Inform: to announce, give information
Delay: late
Cancellation: to cancel, to stop
Platform: place to stand when waiting for a train
Catch the bus or catch the train: an idiom that means to take
Apps: applications to download on mobile phones
Street signs: things we see that gives us directions and instructions
Local Street Signs: gives directions on streets that are small, have lower speed limits, and instructions where people can walk, drive, or ride a bicycle
Highways: high speed roadways that connects cities and towns, have higher speed limits and more traffic
Highway signs: gives directions to drivers or warnings on the highway such as construction and weather warnings
Stop sign: to come to an end; no movement
Bicycles: vehicles that are made of two wheels, a handle bar, and pedals
No bicycles allowed sign: no bicycles permitted on street or sidewalk
Allowed: permit
Sidewalk: a path for people to walk
Closed: a sidewalk or street not open
Traffic: vehicles that move on streets, roads, and highways
Signal Ahead: traffic must prepare to see the signals (red, yellow, green)
Speed limit: restriction of speed on a street
Exit: to leave a street or highway
Push to walk: a button for people to change the light from do not walk to walk
Speed bump: a bump to prevent speeding
Right of way: permission for cars or pedestrians to cross the street
Pedestrians: people
Walk signal: permission to cross the street
Do not walk sign: to stop
Light: the light that instructs pedestrians and cars to go, wait, or stop
Cross: to walk across a street
Jaywalking: to walk across the street without permission
Cyclists: people who ride bicycles
Miles per hour (mph): the amount of speed
Photo enforced: photos taken of cars that break traffic rules
Construction or Work Ahead signs: signs that direct traffic when there is work on the street or highway; these signs are in orange color
Slow sign: to warn drivers to slow down
Flagger: a construction worker that directs traffic when there is work on the road
Detour: change in direction
Work zone: to let drivers know there is construction work ahead
Doctor/physician: a person who examines a patient and writes prescriptions for patients
Patient: a person who visits and receives treatment from a doctor
Appointment: to schedule a time to see the doctor at a doctor's office or hospital
Urgent care: an urgent care center for emergencies; no appointments are necessary

Receptionist: a person who greets patients and schedule appointments

Walk-in: to walk into a clinic without an appointment

Insurance card: a card that states your health insurance; coverage for healthcare and medicine costs

Co-pay: a certain amount of money the patient must pay for a doctor's visit. The health insurance may cover all or some of the medical fees

Pay-out-of-pocket: to pay for doctor services, a fee

Referral: to refer, to send someone to a place for an exam or treatment

Sick: to feel not well; ill

X-ray: an electromagnetic radiation light that can see through parts of the body

Symptoms: feelings of sickness

Fever: to have high temperature; to feel hot and cold

Sore throat: the throat feels irritated, uncomfortable to speak

Cold: to feel sick due to temperature changes in weather

Put you down: to add you to something like a schedule or an appointment

Public restroom: a place to use the bathroom for public use

Stalls: a place for people to use the bathroom privately

Toliet: a basin to relieve yourself

Sink: to wash your hands

Automated sink dispenser: a machine that releases liquid soap

Hand dryer: a machine to air dry hands

Hand dryer with tissue: put hand in front of dryer to automatically release tissue

Rail: helps people who have a difficult time with their balance

HELP button: to alert a medical staff member in an emergency; common in hospitals and doctor's offices

Job: a task, work

Employment: a job, to be employed/hired

Work: to do something or a place of business

Remote: to work from home

Hybrid: to work some days remotely and others in-person

Job search: to find a job

Apply: to request

Job applicants, customers, clients: people who apply for work

Employer: boss, a person in charge of a company or a business

Employee: a person who works for a company or a business

Hire: to receive a job

Job position: the type of job

Full time: to work at least 40 hours a week

Part time: to work less than 40 hours a week

Job requirements: the skills, education, and experience needed for a job position

Skills: things you know how to do

Transferrable skills: the skills you have that can be used towards a job or career

Work experience (also known as *employment history*): types of job positions you had

Resume: an outline of your work experiences, skills, and education

References: people who can talk about your work experience

Salary: money you receive from employer

Job advertisement (also called *ad* or *help wanted*): an announcement about a job position

Abbreviations: short ways of writing words

Job search engine: an online site to find jobs

Job apps (applications): a computer software or program that can be downloaded on computer or phone

Referred: to mention

Find out (found out): to discover information

Interview: a conversation between a client and an employer about the job position the client is applying for

Qualified: to have the requirements for the job position

Interviewer: an employer, the person who conducts an interview

Interviewee: a person applying for a job

Tell me about yourself: to share current or past work experience, skills, and educational background

Strengths: things you are good at

Weakness: things you are not good at or need to improve

Aligned: to give support

Resign: to leave a job position by choice

Laid off: a company closes or a job position ends

Fired: to leave a job position by force

Shopping (to shop): to visit stores to buy items

Refund: to get money back from a purchase (something you bought)

Exchange: to change an item for another one

Receipt: a record of all the things you bought

Store policy: the rules of the store

Customer: a person that buys something

Customer service representative: a person that helps and answers customers' questions

Cashier: a person who calculates (adds up) the costs of customers' items from a register at a supermarket or a store

Price check: the cashier checks the price of an item

Sale: reduced price of items

Salesperson: a person who sells an item or a person who works at a store

Pair of shoes: two shoes

Try on: to try something on your body

Size: how big something is

XS: Extra small

S: Small

M: Medium

L: Large

XL: Extra large

2XL-5XL: Plus sizes

Receipt: a record of all the things you bought

Restaurant: a place to sit in and eat

Café: a small place to sit in and eat or drink coffee or tea

Self-serve: customers make their own coffee or tea and pay at the counter

Diner: a small restaurant

Food truck: a truck or that serves food on the go

Food cart: a cart that serves food on the go

Bakery: a place that serves bread and desserts

Take out: a restaurant that serves food for takeout orders, with or without sit in (example: pizza shop)

Order: to request food or drinks

Cash: money

Fast paced: quick movement

Debit card: a bankcard that you use to make purchases. Money is automatically taken out of bank account when a purchase is made

Credit card: a card used to make purchases. Money is charged to card and payment is due at a certain time

Server: a person who takes an order and serves the customer

Waiter (man)/waitress (woman)/Server: a person who takes an order and serves the customer

Customer: a person who buys something at a store or restaurant

Menu: a list of food and drinks from a restaurant

No substitutions please: cannot substitute one item for another

Dishes: types of food prepared at a restaurant

Appetizers: small dishes to eat before the main course

Main course (also known as *entrees*)**:** the main meal or dish

Meal: something to eat

Dessert: sweet food to eat after a meal

Drinks/Beverages: something to drink (example: coffee, tea, water, juice, soda, alcohol)

Option: to choose

Gratuity (also known as *tip*)**:** additional money given to the server

Yeah: informal way to say *yes*

Lemme: informal way to say *let me*

Coffee: hot drink made from roasted coffee beans

Coffee, light and sweet: coffee with a lot of milk or creamer and sugar

Black coffee: coffee with no milk or creamer, or sugar

Tea: a hot drink made from dried tea leaves that are boiled in hot water

Roll: small loaf of bread

Toast: sliced bread that is heated on both sides making it crispy

Bagel: bread shaped into a ring that is made by boiling the dough and baked

Muffin: small cake that is rounded made from dough or batter

Bacon, egg, and cheese: a type of sandwich made with meat (pork, turkey or beef bacon), cheese (made of pressed curds or milk) and eggs (an oval shaped type of food made from chickens and hens)

APPENDIX C

Answers to exercises

Preview
Colors: write your own answers
Birthday: write your own answers
Time: 9 o'clock or 9:00
Informal English/Slang: write your own answers

UNIT 1-Inside a House

Matching: b. TV, c. and d. table and chairs, a. refrigerator

Prepositions of place
1. next to living room, across from bedroom 1
2. next to kitchen, across from bedroom 2
3. next to bedroom 1
4. next to bedroom 2

Excuse me, where is your bathroom?
Daisey is at Sasha's house
Sasha gave Daisey a glass of water
The bathroom is down the hallway on the left

I'll be right back means to return/come back soon

TRUE of FALSE
1. True 2. False 3. False 4. True

Would you eat or drink from this kitchen? Why?
Write your own answer

Let's talk about dishes: name the utensils and utensils used for dishes
Butter knife, knife, salad-**fork**, chicken with noodles, and vegetables-**fork or spoon**, coffee-**cup, teaspoon**, fruit-**fork or spoon**, wine-**glass**, bagels-**butter knife**

Which of these foods you **DO NOT** need to use an utensil?
A. Hummus- write your own answer
B. Pizza- write your own answer

UNIT 2-Let's Cook!

Match the letters with the correct picture
Pot- A, Frying pan- B, D, Not a pot or frying pan-C

<u>Matching</u>
1. Muffin pan, 2. Spatula, 3. Pot, 4. Measuring cup, 5. Aluminum pan, 6. Fry
7. Boil, 8. Whisk, 9. Bake

<u>Let's bake a cake-answer the questions</u>
Anika wants to eat cake
Anika needs an aluminum pan
TRUE or FALSE: 1. True, 2. False

<u>TRUE or FALSE</u>
True, False, True, False, False

<u>Why is it important to check the cake with a fork before taking it out the oven?</u>
To make sure it's cooked thoroughly

UNIT 3-Supermarket Food Labels and Circulars

Write your list

<u>Read the label and answer the questions</u>
1. $4.99
2. chicken
3. fruit punch
4. get 2 items for 1 price

<u>TRUE or FALSE</u>
1. True, 2. True, 3. False

<u>Read circular advertisement and questions</u>
1. peppers, cantaloupes, and oranges
2. $3.99
3. cantaloupes
4. pound
5. black and blueberries, romaine hearts, white mushrooms, cucumbers, salads

<u>What items should you buy?</u> Write your own answer

UNIT 4-Transportation

<u>What time should person A catch the bus?</u>
Person A should catch the bus

<u>Read the bus schedule and answer the questions</u>
1. Madison Ave, 2. 2:30, 3. 10th street, 4. No, there are no buses arriving at 10th street
until 4:10, 5. Take the 2:40 bus at Brick Avenue

"There are no trains going to 25 street, Day street and Penny Avenue. Take the shuttle bus at 93-96 Boulevard to get to those stops."

Conversation between the train clerk and the customer
1. Take next train to 93-96 boulevard and catch shuttle bus to Penny Ave.
2. Wait for the 1:05 train to get to Day Street
3. Take the train one stop to 93-96 boulevard and take the shuttle bus to Penny Ave.

UNIT 5-Local Street and Highway Signs

Matching: 1. **I**, 2. **F**, 3. **B**, 4. **H**, 5. **A**, 6. **E**, 7. **D**, 8. **C**, 9. **G**

TRUE or FALSE: 1. FALSE, 2. TRUE

Look at the signs and answer the questions
1. **6**, 2. **Picture 1**, 3. **B**, 4. **Exit, highway signs**, 5. **A, B, C**, 6. **B, C**, 7. **A, B**

UNIT 6-Doctor verses Hospital Appointments

Making a doctor's appointment
1. Feels sick, head hurts, feels hot all the time
2. One week ago
3. Tomorrow at 9 am
4. No
5. $75.00

Making a hospital appointment
1. Doctor referral
2. X-ray
3. Metal will interfere with X-ray exam, dangerous
4. Dr. Julie West

Where do you go to see the doctor? Why?
Write your own answer

Health insurance card
1. ABC Health Insurance
2. Stephen Joseph
3. 3/19/1979
4. $35.00
5. Dr. Joy Heart

Conversation between patient and doctor TRUE or FALSE:
1. TRUE, 2. FALSE, 3. FALSE, 4. TRUE, 5. FALSE, 6. TRUE

UNIT 7-Public Restroom

Do you go to a public restroom? Where do you go to use a public restroom?
Write your own answers

Read the conversation and answer the questions
1. Bay Park
2. Are there any restrooms close by?
3. False

Which dryer do you prefer?
Write your own answer

Knock Knock...is anyone there? Conversation and questions

1. What is the difference between conversation 1 and 2?
Conversation 1-someone knocks on the door and asks is anyone there
Conversation 2-person A fell on the floor

2. Why did the nurse come into the bathroom stall?
Person A fell on the floor and couldn't get up

3. Why is it important to knock on the stall?
It's respectful to knock to see if someone is inside a stall

UNIT 8-What kind of job do you want?

Name the job you want or would like to have?
Write your own answers

Why do you want these jobs?
Write your own answer

Job versus Career chart
Complete the chart with your own answers

What careers are you interested in? Why?
Write your own answers

Read the job ad about temporary work and answer the questions
Write your own answers

Read the job ads and answer the questions
1. Front desk attendant and Front desk security
2. up to $22/hour
3. call the phone number

4. FALSE

Match the word with its abbreviation
a. P/T
b. req
c. exp
d. res

What would you prefer (remote, hybrid, or in-person work)?
Write your own answer

Transferrable skills
Write your own answer

What transferrable skills do you have to apply for the job?
Write your own answer

UNIT 9-Let's go Shopping!

I want a refund! Conversation: Do you think the customer should get a refund? Why?
Write your own answer

What is your size? What is your shoe size?
Write your own answers

What is your favorite clothing?
Circle your answers

What is Teacher Dara wearing?
Picture 1: coat, pants, shoes
Picture 2: jacket, jeans, sneakers
Picture 3: dress, sandals
Picture 4: t-shirt, skirt

Read the ad and answer the questions
1. Men's shirts, women's dresses and jackets
2. Sale ends
3. Pair of men's pants
4. Not after the sale is over

Conversation between the customer and salesperson
1. The customer wants a shirt in size 2XL

Conversation between the customer and salesperson about shoes and sneakers
1. The customer wants a size 8 in shoes and 8 ½ in sneakers
2. There are no size 8 shoes available, only have size 10

UNIT 10-Going out to eat
Answer the question from the conversations

1. Chicken and rice dish, salad and wine
2. Large coffee light and sweet, a toasted bagel with butter
3. A restaurant is a place to sit, order food to eat inside or to takeout. A coffee cart is a fast-food restaurant to order food, pay and leave
4. Write your own answer

You Try: Write a conversation between a customer and a server
Write your own answer

PREVIEW LESSON WORKSHEETS

Complete the alphabet chart

A		C	D			G	H		J
	L	M	N		P		R		T
U		W		Z					

Write the number

1 _____

2 _____

3 _____

4 _____

5 _____

6 _____

Write the lower case letter

A	B	C	D	E	F	G	H	I	J
K	L	M	N	O	P	Q	R	S	T
U	V	W	X	Y	Z				

Write the number

10 _____

20 _____

30 _____

40 _____

50 _____

Look at the calendars and write the date

MARCH 2024

Sunday	Monday	Tuesday	Wednesday	Thursday	Friday	Saturday
					1	2
3	4	5	6	(7)	8	9
10	11	12	13	14	15	16
17	18	19	20	21	22	23
24	25	26	27	28	29	30
31						

_____

APRIL 2024

Sunday	Monday	Tuesday	Wednesday	Thursday	Friday	Saturday
	1	2	3	4	5	6
7	8	9	10	11	12	13
14	15	16	17	18	19	20
21	22	23	24	(25)	26	27
28	29	30				

_____

Days of the week: Fill in the blanks

M ____ n ____ ____ y

____ u ____ s ____ a ____

W ____ ____ ____ e s ____ a ____

____ h u ____ s ____ ____ ____

F ____ i d ____ ____

S ____ ____ u ____ d a ____

____ ____ ____ d ____ ____

Write the abbreviation

Monday _____   Friday _____

Tuesday _____   Saturday _____

Wednesday _____   Sunday _____

Thursday _____

Months of the year: Write the month

Jan _____ Jul _____

Feb _____ Aug _____

Mar _____ Sept _____

Apr _____ Oct _____

May _____ Nov _____

Jun _____ Dec _____

Write the correct month for each sentence

The <u>first</u> month of the year is _____

The <u>third</u> month of the year is _____

The <u>fifth</u> month of the year is _____

The <u>seventh</u> month of the year is _____

The <u>ninth</u> month of the year is _____

The <u>eleventh</u> month of the year is _____

What is today?

Write the date using ordinals

JULY 2024

Sunday	Monday	Tuesday	Wednesday	Thursday	Friday	Saturday
	1	2	3	4	5	6
7	8	9	10	11	12	13
14	15	16	17	18	19	20
21	22	23	24	25	26	27
28	29	30	31			

Today is _____

AUGUST 2024

Sunday	Monday	Tuesday	Wednesday	Thursday	Friday	Saturday
				1	2	3
4	5	6	7	8	9	10
11	12	13	14	15	16	17
18	19	20	21	22	23	24
25	26	27	28	29	30	31

Today is _____

What is today?

Write the date using ordinals

SEPTEMBER 2024

Sunday	Monday	Tuesday	Wednesday	Thursday	Friday	Saturday
1	2	3	4	5	6	7
8	9	10	11	12	13	14
15	16	17	18	19	20	21
22	23	24	25	26	27	28
29	30					

Today is _____

OCTOBER 2024

Sunday	Monday	Tuesday	Wednesday	Thursday	Friday	Saturday
		1	2	3	4	5
6	7	8	9	10	11	12
13	14	15	16	17	18	19
20	21	22	23	24	25	26
27	28	29	30	31		

Today is _____

What is the season?

_____

_____

_____

_____

Choose the correct words to describe the weather

Rainy Hot Cold Cloudy Sunny Foggy Warm Cool

It is

It is

It is

It is

Use the words to describe the weather in the picture

| Hot   Cold   Sunny   Snowy   Warm   Cool |

Write the name of the holiday and month

Name of holiday

_____

Month

_____

Write the name of the holiday and month

Name of holiday

_____

Month

_____

Write the name of the holiday and the month

Name of holiday

_____

Month

_____

Which picture is birthday?

1. _____

2. _____

Which picture is Thanksgiving?

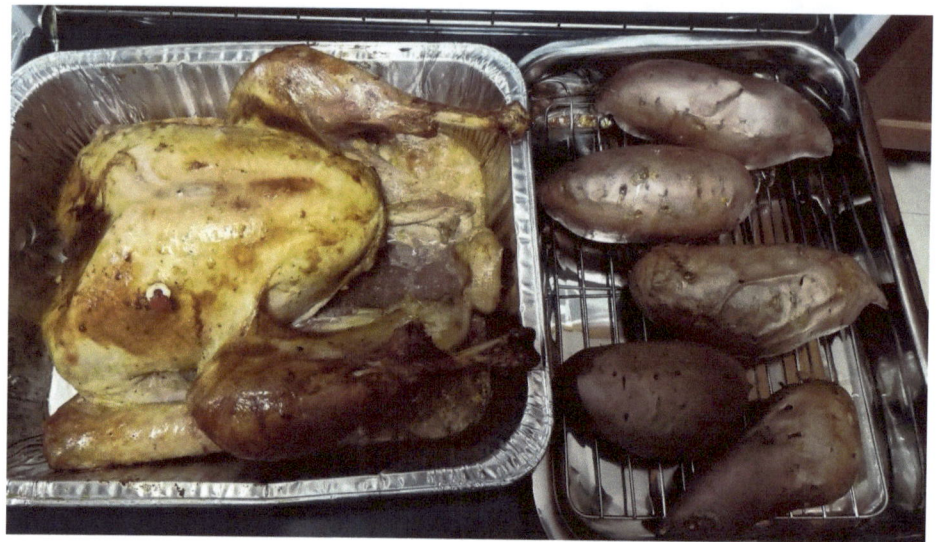

1. _____

2. _____

What time is it?

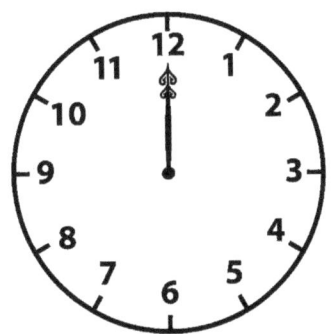

It is _____

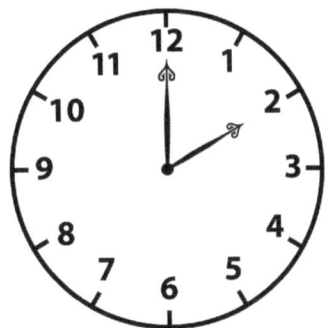

It is _____

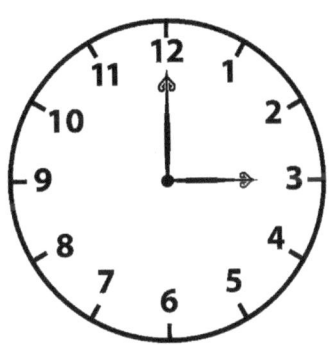

It is _____

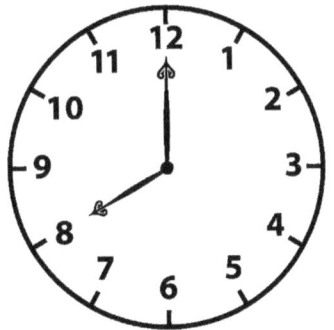

It is _____

What time is it?

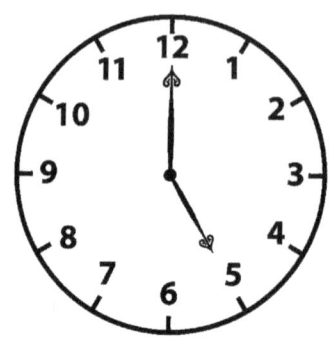

It is _____

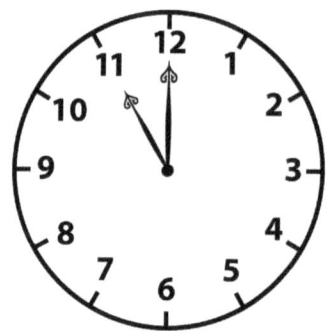

It is _____

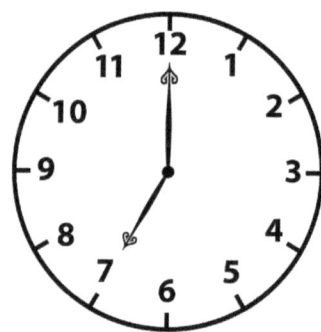

It is _____

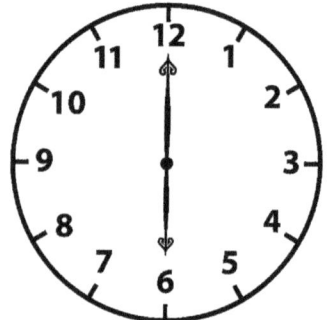

It is _____

Draw the time

Teacher Dara says:

TRY YOUR BEST